RECONCILIATION
A CHANGE OF HEART

Mary Cay Senger

THE LITURGICAL PRESS
St. John's Abbey
Collegeville, MN 56321

Acknowledgments

Photography

Bets Anderson Bailly, pg. 29 (left)

Bob Brinkley & Marcia Simpson, pg. 12

CLEO, pg. v (right), pp. 14 (bottom), 20 (right), 21, 25 (top)

Alan Cliburn, pg. 26 (top, left)

Vivienne della Grotta, pg. 29 (right)

Gail Denham, pg. 33

Joseph Di Chello, pg. 3 (bottom)

Roberta Donovan, pp. v (bottom), 39

Doranne Jacobson, pp. 20 (left), 26 (bottom left)

Jean Libby, pg. 17 (right)

Dennis MacDonald, pg. 57

Marjorie Masel, pg. 3 (top)

Tom McGuire, pp. 14 (top), 49

James Mejuto, pg. 5 (bottom)

Alan Oddie, cover (bottom right), pp. 7, 10, 17 (bottom left), 20 (top), 30, 31, 35, 57

Rob Outlaw, cover (top left), pg. 25 (bottom)

Robert Paulson, pp. 17 (top left), 50

Cyril Reilly, pg. 17 (top right)

Will & Angie Rumpf, pp. v (top), 46

Jim Shaffer, cover (top), pp. 18, 23, 61, 65, 71

Bob Taylor, cover (bottom left), pp. 1, 26 (right)

Betty Hurwich Zoss, pp. v (left), 5 (top), 9

Illustrations

Monica Bokinskie, pp. 34, 45, 48

Ruth Landry, pp. 38, 43

Janice St. Marie, pp. 13, 24, 28, 32, 51, 54, 55, 90

The Author: Mary Cay Senger is the director of adult and family education for St. Joseph's Parish, Mandan, North Dakota.

Note: The "Lesson Helps," pp. 77–86, and the "Suggested Badges," pg. 90, may be photocopied for use with this book without further permission of The Liturgical Press.

Nihil obstat: Rev. Robert C. Harren, J.C.L., *Censor deputatus.*

Imprimatur: ✠ George H. Speltz, D.D., Apostolic Administrator, Diocese of St. Cloud, Minnesota. March 31, 1987.

CONTENTS

INTRODUCTION

Reconciliation—A Change of Heart is addressed primarily to the second- or third-grade child preparing to receive the Sacrament of Reconciliation for the first time. It also involves the child's parents or other principal care-givers and the parish religious education teachers in the preparation process. Four lessons are for use in a classroom setting, and four are for use at home during a time of parent-child sharing.

This book introduces the child to the Commandments, the Beatitudes, and the Works of Mercy—all ways of living according to God's laws of love. The child will study these topics further as his or her instruction in the Catholic faith continues at home or through school and parish religious education programs. In working with *Reconciliation—A Change of Heart,* the child will have opportunities to memorize some basic material about this sacrament and the faith. This, however, should not be the criterion that determines a child's readiness for the Sacrament of Reconciliation.

While eight lessons may seem to be a long preparation for this sacrament, it is important that the child take sufficient time to build a positive foundation of certain truths of our Catholic faith and the Christian way of life. Such a foundation includes an understanding that

—we belong to God's family and we are good.

—we have many ways to grow in this goodness. The Commandments, Beatitudes, and Works of Mercy help us in this growth.

—we sometimes turn away from living according to these Commandments, Beatitudes, and Works of Mercy. We need a change of heart.

—we can become reconciled with one another and with God. We celebrate this conversion through the Sacrament of Reconciliation.

—the Sacrament of Reconciliation can be a profound, joy-filled experience of forgiveness and peace of heart.

Reconciliation—A Change of Heart offers the parents or other care-givers who attend the parent sessions and who prepare the children in the home sessions an opportunity to develop a "celebration outlook" toward reconciliation. These adults, along with the children, will learn that conversion of heart can take place in the lives of all who seek reconciliation through this sacrament.

Mary Cay Senger

I Belong to the Family of God

I am alive!
I can run,
    eat,
      play,
and help others.

**Thank you, God,
for the gift
of life!**

Here is an announcement
about my birth:

NEWS! NEWS! NEWS!

_____

_____

_____

_____

Many people were glad I
was born. Their names are:

_____

_____

_____

_____

I am a good person.
I have talents that make
me special.

**Thank you, God, for the talents
that you have given to me!**

TALENT SEARCH

GENTLE

FRIENDLY

PEACEFUL

CHEERFUL

CALM

TRUTHFUL

KIND

GOOD

LOVING

HELPFUL

PRAYERFUL

UNSELFISH

FUNNY

FORGIVING

Find and circle in the puzzle the talent words listed above:

```
P U N S E L F I S H P A
T R U T H F U L P B E F
C J A G E N T L E Y A O
H S C Y J D O O G L C R
E E A L E N K I N D E G
E K L D M R W R I N F I
R C M P K G F H V E U V
F Q T D F Y S U O I L I
U Z K L P U F N L R O N
L F U N N Y L Z R F E G
```

I belong to a family.
My family is special.

**Thank you, God,
for my family!**

My family does these activities
together:

_____

_____

_____

_____

Find the hidden message by matching
the letters with the numbers found
below the lines:

A B C D E F G H I J K L M
1 2 3 4 5 6 7 8 9 10 11 12 13

N O P Q R S T U V W X Y Z
14 15 16 17 18 19 20 21 22 23 24 25 26

___ ___ ___   ___ ___ ___ ___ ___
 7   15   4   12 15 22   5 19

___ ___ ___ ___   ___ ___ ___ ___ ___ ___
 5   1   3   8   16   5 18 19 15 14

___ ___   ___ ___   ___ ___ ___ ___ ___ ___
 9 14   13 25   6   1 13   9 12 25

I became
a member of
the Church
when I was
baptized.

I belong to the
family of God.

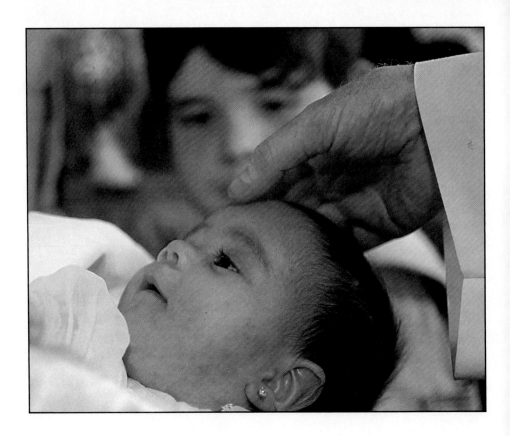

Find the correct word to complete each
sentence. Then, match the word to the same
sentence number found in the crossword puzzle:

church   baptized
talents   life
special   together
Catholic

1. (across) I am a s_____ person.

2. (down) I was b_____ into
         God's family.

3. (down) I am a member of the
         C_____ Church.

4. (across) I have many t_____.

5. (down) My family does many
         activities t_____.

6. (across) I have the gift of l_____.

7. (across) Most babies are baptized
         in c_____.

I want to be a good member
of God's family, so I pray:

Write a prayer asking God to help you grow in goodness and love in the
family of God:

Dear God, _____

_____

_____

_____

_____

_____

_____

_____

_____

_____

_____

_____

_____

I Live as a Child of God

My family took me to church
to be baptized.

**The priest or the deacon prayed,
"I baptize you**

_____

**in the name of the Father, and
of the Son, and of the
Holy Spirit."**

Here is a picture of my baptism:

My godparents are:

_____

_____

Many people came to celebrate
my baptism. Their names are:

_____

_____

_____

_____

Because of my baptism I can
CELEBRATE God's life
and love within me!

I can bring God's love to other people.

**Thank you, God,
for your life
and love.**

We Bring God's Love to Others

Parent hugs a child. Move ahead 4.

Children argue and fight. Move back 1.

START

Use a die (or a set of cards, turned face down, numbered 1–6). Throw the die or turn up a number card to move the markers (buttons, chips, etc.) from START to A HAPPY HOME. Follow the directions when you land on a message:

Child shares a favorite toy. Take another turn.

Children send a card to a sick friend. Move ahead 1.

Child lies to parent. Move back 5.

Child cleans room. Move ahead 2.

The family prays together. Move ahead 4.

Everyone helps to clean the yard. Move ahead 3.

Parent gets angry. Move back 7.

A HAPPY HOME

Child makes fun of someone. Skip a turn.

Family members love and forgive. Move into your happy home.

Sometimes I am selfish or unkind.
Sometimes I do not show love
to my family or to my friends.

I can tell them, "I am sorry."

**Dear God,
Thank you for family
and friends who love me
and forgive me.**

Color the squares YELLOW that show a
person loving God and others. Color the
squares GREEN that show a person who
needs to say, "I am sorry."

I do not listen.	I do not obey.	I am kind to others.	I am selfish.	I hurt a friend.
I am selfish.	I cheat at school.	I help a friend.	I do not listen.	I make fun of someone.
I show respect.	I share my things.	I pray for my family.	I tell the truth.	I obey my teachers.
I stay angry with my parents.	I hurt a friend.	I praise God in church.	I make fun of someone.	I tell a lie.
I cheat at school.	I do not listen.	I am good at home.	I cheat at school.	I am selfish.
I tell a lie.	I am selfish.	I help a neighbor.	I do not obey.	I hurt a friend.
I do not obey.	I do not tell the truth.	I clean up my room.	I stay angry with my parents.	I do not listen.

Family Prayer Time

Parent	**Dear God,** **We thank you for loving each one of us.** **We belong to you. We are happy to be** **members of your family. Please help us** **to show love for one another. Teach us to** **reach out to each other with forgiving** **hearts.** Each member of the family shares one way that he or she has shown love or goodness during the past day or days. Then he or she lights a candle.
Family members (after each sharing)	**"Let us give thanks to God."** Each member of the family shares one way that he or she did not show enough love during the past day or days. Then, he or she blows out his or her candle and says, "I am sorry."
Family members (after each sharing)	**"We ask your forgiveness, Lord."**
All	**Dear God,** **We love you. We praise your goodness to us.** **We ask you to forgive us our sins. Bring us** **closer to you and to one another. Help us to let** **the light of our goodness shine before others.** Relight each candle.
Parent	**Let us remember all the members of our** **world-wide family as we pray together,** **"Our Father . . ."**
All	Sing a favorite song, such as: "This Little Light of Mine," "I've Got the Joy," "Peace Is Flowing Like a River."
All	Enjoy a popcorn party or some other favorite treat.

The Commandments
Numbers 1–5

My family has rules.
Rules can help make our home a
happy place. Rules help us think
about others.

These rules are good for my family:

1. _____

2. _____

3. _____

4. _____

_____

_____

The family of God has rules.
These rules can help us to love and
care for one another.

They are called the "Ten Commandments"
or the "Ten Words of God."

1. I am the Lord, your God.
   Do not have other gods.

2. Do not misuse God's name.

3. Keep holy the Lord's Day.

4. Honor your parents.

5. Do not harm yourself or others.

6. Be faithful to your husband or wife.

7. Do not steal.

8. Do not lie.

9. Do not covet someone's husband or wife.

10. Do not covet someone's goods.

1 First Commandment:

I am the Lord, your God.
Do not have other gods.

Sometimes God is not important to us.
We can make other things more
important than God.

**Dear God,
Help me to put you first
in my life.**

2 Second Commandment

Do not misuse God's name.

There is no one greater than God.
God's name is holy.

Sometimes we do not respect God's name.
We use it in anger or in a careless way.

Dear God,
Help me to use your name
with love and respect.

Find and circle in this puzzle these names for God:

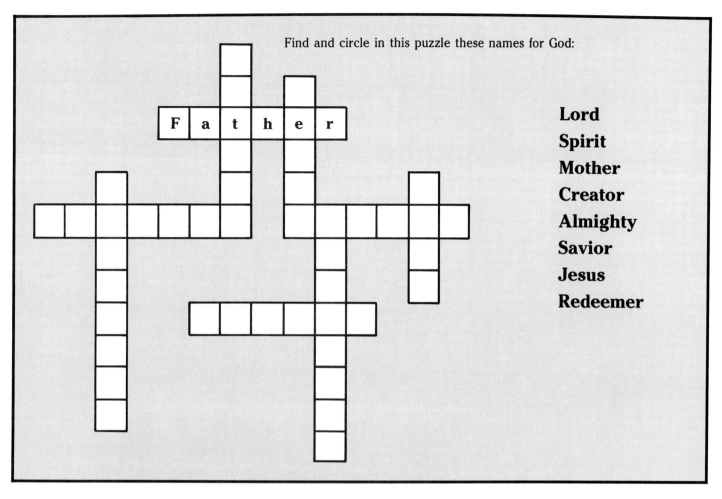

F a t h e r

Lord
Spirit
Mother
Creator
Almighty
Savior
Jesus
Redeemer

Find the Commandment message by matching the letters with
the numbers found below the lines:

A	B	C	D	E	F	G	H	I	J	K	L	M
1	2	3	4	5	6	7	8	9	10	11	12	13
N	O	P	Q	R	S	T	U	V	W	X	Y	Z
14	15	16	17	18	19	20	21	22	23	24	25	26

___ ___ ___   ___ ___   ___ ___ ___ ___ ___   ___ ___
 7   15   4   9   19   6   9   18 19   20   9   14

___ ___   ___ ___ ___ ___   ___   ___ ___ ___ ___   ___ ___ ___
13   25   12   9   6   5   9   23   9   12   12   14   15   20 .

___ ___ ___ ___   ___ ___ ___ ___ ___   ___ ___ ___ ___ ___ ___
13   1   11   5   15   20   8   5   18   20   8   9   14   7   19

___ ___ ___ ___   ___ ___ ___ ___ ___ ___ ___ ___ ___   ___ ___ ___ ___
13   15   18   5   9   13   16   15   18   20   1   14   20   20   8   1   14

___ ___ ___ .
 7   15   4

22

3 Third Commandment

Keep holy the Lord's Day.

Sunday is a special day to help us
keep God first in our lives.

We can use Sunday to:

- Go to church to give thanks to our God
  who loves us

- Read from the Bible or other books
  about God

- Take time to enjoy the beauty of nature

- Relax and enjoy our family and friends

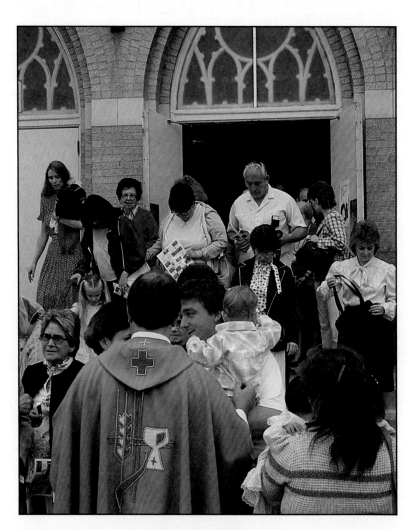

Find your way to the church to give
thanks to our God:

4 Fourth Commandment

Honor your parents.

The love of parents is life-giving.
They love us into goodness, truthfulness,
wonder, and service to others.

Parents need our love, our respect, our prayers.

Thank you, God, for my parents, grandparents, teachers, and all others who bring me closer to you.

5 Fifth Commandment

Do not harm yourself or others.

Life is God's gift to us.
We must take care of our own lives
and the lives of others.
We cannot let hate, anger, or fear
control us.

Dear God,
Thank you for life!
Help me take care
of my own life.
Help me respect life
in everyone and in
everything around me.

We respect our parents.

In this space draw or paste pictures from magazines that show people treating each other with love and respect.

We respect life. We respect our parents.

We respect life. We respect our parents.

We respect life.

We respect life.

Zacchaeus did not respect
his own life or the
lives of others.
Money was more important
to him than God.
Then he met Jesus.
Jesus showed him love
and forgiveness.
Zacchaeus changed his life
and kept God's laws with
an unselfish, loving heart.

**Dear God,
Help me to change my heart.
Help me to become
unselfish and loving.**

The Commandments
Numbers 6–10

6 Sixth Commandment

Be faithful to your husband or wife.

When a man and woman get married, they promise to love each other. When they keep this promise, they are *faithful* to each other.

We can be faithful to family members and friends.

**Dear God,
Help me to treat each person with
respect. Help me learn to be faithful,
to keep my promises.**

Circle the words below that will help
you be a faithful friend:

forgiving	truthful
understanding	stealing
selfish	funny
prayerful	lying
respectful	making fun of
peaceful	helpful
unkind	friendly
angry	loving
thankful	stubborn

Try to put the words below in a different order
to make a sentence about a faithful friend:

you When find a friend faithful find you a treasure.

7 Seventh Commandment
Do not steal.

We steal from someone when we take something that does not belong to us.

When we steal answers in school, we call it "cheating."

When we steal things in a store, we call it "shoplifting."

**Dear God,
Help me to keep
stealing out of
my life.**

Help the child return the book to the store
by finding the hidden path in the maze:

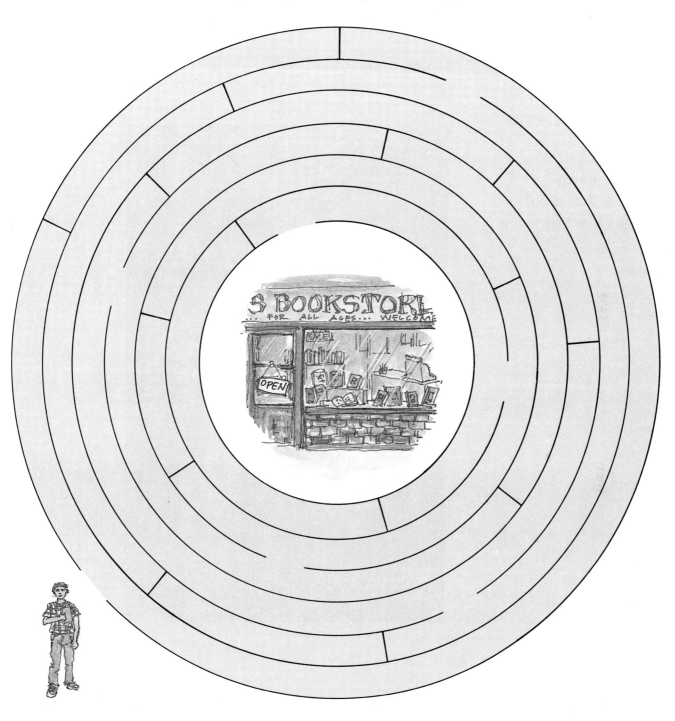

8 Eighth Commandment
Do not lie.

Sometimes we do not tell the truth.
We call this *lying*.

Other people want us to tell the truth.
They want to believe what we say.

**Dear God,
Help me to tell
the truth, even
when it is hard for
me to be honest.**

Connect each set of circles and triangles
to find a word that means "truthful":

9 Ninth Commandment

Do not covet someone's husband or wife.

10 Tenth Commandment

Do not covet someone's goods.

To "covet" means to want something so much
that we start to plan how to take it away
from someone else.
We try to think of a way to steal it.

Dear God,
Help me to be thankful
for the things I have.
Help me not to covet
what belongs to someone else.

TRUE-FALSE Statements on the Commandments

The Ten Commandments teach us to:

_____	make Sunday a special day
_____	tell lies
_____	hurt our friends
_____	respect our parents
_____	take good care of our own lives
_____	tell the truth
_____	steal from a store
_____	be happy with the good things we have
_____	have only one God
_____	use God's name with respect
_____	cheat in school
_____	be faithful to family and friends

Identify the Ten Commandments by number:

1   _____Do not steal.

2   _____Keep holy the Lord's Day.

3   _____Do not kill.

4   _____I am the Lord, your God. Do not have other gods.

5   _____Do not covet someone's goods.

6   _____Do not misuse God's name.

7   _____Honor your parents.

8   _____Do not covet someone's husband or wife.

9   _____Be faithful to your husband or wife.

10   _____Do not lie.

Family Prayer Time

Family member

**Dear Jesus,
You showed us how to love others. Help our
family to show our love for one another.**

Each member of the family shares one way that
he or she has shown love or goodness during the
past day or days.

Family members
(after each sharing)

"Thank you for the gift of love."

Each member shares one way that he or she did not
share enough love.

Family members
(after each sharing)

"We are sorry, Lord."

As a family fill in the sections of the heart:

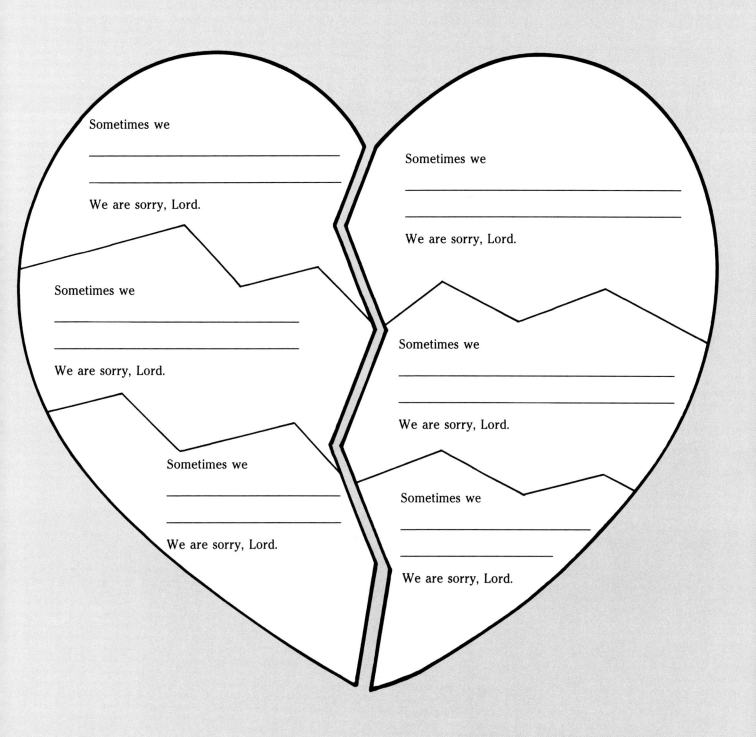

Sometimes we

_____

_____

We are sorry, Lord.

Sometimes we

_____

_____

We are sorry, Lord.

Sometimes we

_____

_____

We are sorry, Lord.

Sometimes we

_____

_____

We are sorry, Lord.

Sometimes we

_____

_____

We are sorry, Lord.

Sometimes we

_____

_____

We are sorry, Lord.

All   **Lord, help us to heal the brokenness in our family. Teach us to love. Amen.**

All   Enjoy a favorite treat or activity.

38

The Beatitudes: "Happy are they . . . ."

Jesus taught the people many ways
to live the Commandments.
He told the people they could become
blessed and happy if they lived as
he taught.

He said:

- Happy are the poor in the spirit.

- Happy are the gentle.

- Happy are those who mourn.

- Happy are those who hunger and thirst for what is right.

- Happy are the merciful.

- Happy are the pure in heart.

- Happy are the peacemakers.

- Happy are those who suffer as they protect and defend

what is right.

The reward for this kind of living
is the Kingdom of Heaven where each person
can see God face-to-face.

Happy are the poor in spirit.
The Kingdom of Heaven is theirs.

The poor in spirit depend on God.

Color the boxes below that tell how a person can be poor in spirit:

Do not depend on God.	Be angry.	Be unselfish.	Give thanks for God's gifts of love.	Do not show respect.	Do not pray.	Do not obey grandparents.
Be selfish.	Pray to God.	Talk back to your parents.	Try to live God's laws.	Hurt someone's feelings.	Steal someone's coat.	Make fun of our bodies.
Tell lies.	Hit someone.	Steal from a store.	Use money to help the poor.	Say unkind things about others.	Refuse to copy someone's answers in school.	Do not tell the truth.
Do not obey parents.	Make fun of others.	Act silly in church.	Do not take care of your health.	Do not obey city laws.	Do not obey your teacher.	Never pray to God.
Do not go to church.	Use God's name with respect.	Be generous with others.	Share food, clothes, money.	Visit a sick friend.	Hurt your neighbor.	Laugh at others because they are different.
Steal someone's toy.	Make money more important than God.	Hope in God.	Believe in God's love.	Ask only for what we need.	Remember God's love for us.	Pray for each other.

Happy are the gentle.
They shall be children of the earth.

When I am gentle, I am:

g _____

e _____

n _____

t _____

l _____

e _____

From the list below (or from elsewhere) choose a favorite word or words
to show gentleness for each of the lines above. Match your word
or words with the letter at the beginning of each line:

good	not angry	thankful
nice to others	tender	not hurtful
loving	enthusiastic	encouraging
grateful	eager to help	gracious

42

Happy are those who mourn.
They shall find comfort.

Color the flowers that show where we can find
God's healing and peace of heart:

**Happy are those who hunger
and thirst for what is right.
They shall be satisfied.**

Find the Beatitude message by matching the letters with
the numbers found below the lines:

A B C D E F G H I J K L M
1 2 3 4 5 6 7 8 9 10 11 12 13

N O P Q R S T U V W X Y Z
14 15 16 17 18 19 20 21 22 23 24 25 26

— —   — — —   — — — —   — — — — — —
9 6   25 15 21   12 15 22 5   15 20 8 5 18 19

— — —   — — — —   — — —   — — — —
25 15 21   23 9 12 12   14 15 20   8 1 18 13

— — — — .   — —   — — — —   — —   — —
20 8 5 13   20 15   12 15 22 5   9 19   20 15

— — — —   — — —   — — — — —   — — —
15 2 5 25   20 8 5   23 8 15 12 5   12 1 23

— —   — — —
15 6   7 15 4

Happy are the merciful.
They will receive mercy from others.

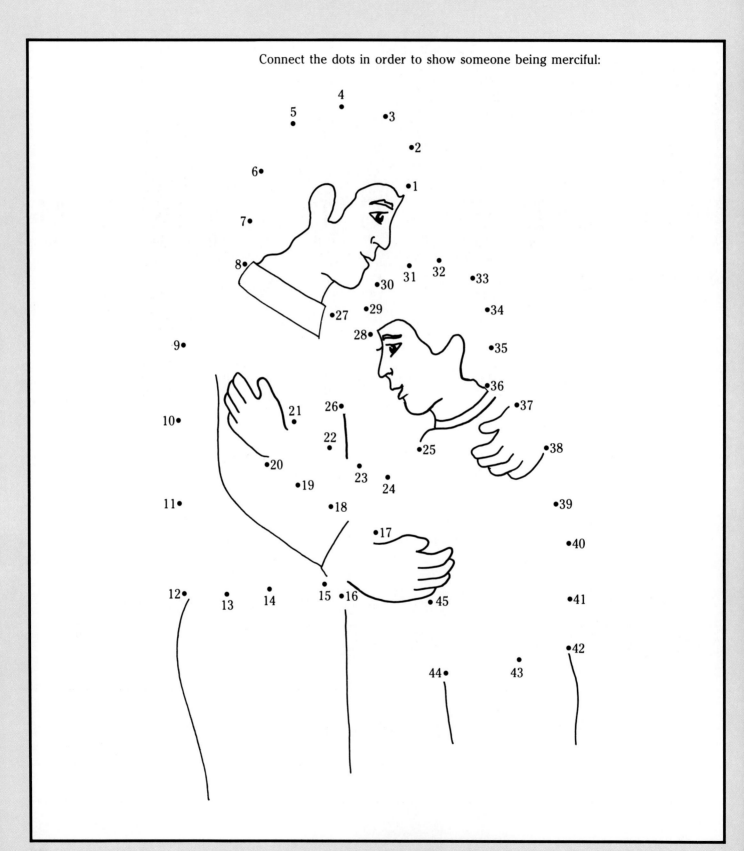

Connect the dots in order to show someone being merciful:

Happy are the pure in heart.
They shall see God.

The pure in heart know that God is
present within them.

They try to see themselves as God sees them.

These are some good things God sees in me:

_____

_____

_____

_____

_____

**Happy are the peacemakers.
They shall be called sons and daughters
of God.**

Draw a picture of a place where you can be a peacemaker:

Happy are they who suffer for doing
what is right.
The Kingdom of Heaven belongs to them.

Sometimes it is hard to do the right thing.
Jesus did what was right, but he
still had to carry a cross.

Sometimes I carry my own kind of cross.
Here is one way I carry a cross.

On the lines in the cross, write
one way that you find difficult in
living as God wants you to live:

**Dear God,
Help me to carry
my cross
with love.**

The Works of Mercy: We Serve One Another

Jesus taught us how to serve
one another. He said:

"Feed the hungry.
Give drink to the thirsty.
Clothe the naked.
Visit the sick.
Visit those in prison.
Shelter those without a home.
Bury those who die."

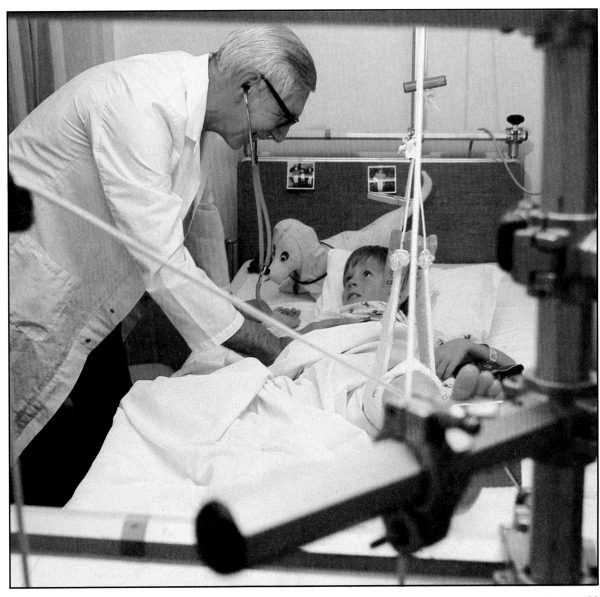

Jesus Feeds the Hungry

Once, when Jesus was teaching a
crowd of more than five thousand, he
noticed that the people were hungry.
He asked his apostles to find food for them.
The apostles said that there was not enough
food on hand for so many people.

The Apostle Andrew did find a boy who had
two fish and five loaves of bread. The boy was
willing to share this food with the people.

Jesus then prayed, blessed the fish and bread,
and asked the apostles to hand out the food
to the hungry crowd. To the apostles' surprise,
twelve baskets full of bread and fish were left over.
John 6:1-14

We have hungry people, thirsty people,
and homeless people today.
Here is a picture I found of some
very poor people:

In this space paste a photo from a newspaper or a magazine
showing people in need:

**Dear Jesus,
Help me to reach out to the poor
whenever I can. Teach me your ways.**

Jesus said:
"When you have a feast, invite the beggars,
the crippled, the lame, and the blind.
You should be glad that they cannot repay you,
for you will be repaid in heaven."

Luke 14:13-14

I can help the hungry, the thirsty,
the homeless by . . .

Complete the sentence above by checking "yes" or "no" to the phrases in each box.
(*Yes* if it is a way to help the needy. *No* if it is not a way to help the needy.):

putting some of my own money into the Sunday collection. _____ ☐ yes ☐ no	buying more toys for myself. _____ ☐ yes ☐ no	learning to share my things at home. _____ ☐ yes ☐ no	praying for the needy. _____ ☐ yes ☐ no
expecting to be paid every time I help someone. _____ ☐ yes ☐ no	helping someone who cannot afford to pay for my work. _____ ☐ yes ☐ no	helping my family fix a food basket for a poor person. _____ ☐ yes ☐ no	making fun of someone who cannot afford nice clothes. _____ ☐ yes ☐ no

Find it in the Bible!

Match the Gospel passage (A) with the message about someone being healed by Jesus (B):

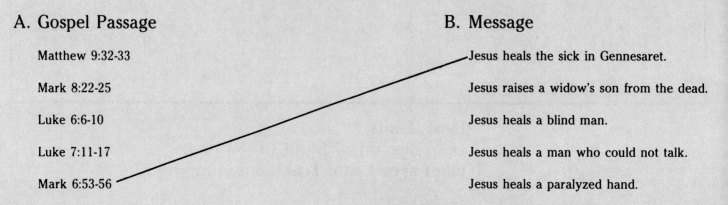

A. Gospel Passage

Matthew 9:32-33

Mark 8:22-25

Luke 6:6-10

Luke 7:11-17

Mark 6:53-56

B. Message

Jesus heals the sick in Gennesaret.

Jesus raises a widow's son from the dead.

Jesus heals a blind man.

Jesus heals a man who could not talk.

Jesus heals a paralyzed hand.

Jesus Visits the Sick

Sick people, the lonely, and worried people knew that Jesus was their friend.

Once, when Jesus was out walking, ten men with a disease called leprosy came to him. These men had sores all over their bodies. They asked Jesus to make them well.

Jesus cured them. Their bodies no longer had the ugly sores.

They all went away happy. Only one man came back to Jesus and thanked him.

Luke 17:11-19

I can be like Jesus.
I can . . . .

To find the message begin with the letter "V." Then, moving to the right, copy down every other letter on the lines below:

Family Prayer Time

Family member	**Dear God,** **We know you love us. Help us to reach out** **to share love with those who need us.**
Family member	Reads from the Bible—Matthew 25:31-40
	Each family member shares one way he or she has shown love and kindness.
Family members (after each sharing)	**Whatever we do to others,** **we do to you, O Lord.**
	Each family member shares one way he or she has hurt someone instead of helping them.
Family members (after each sharing)	**Whatever we do to others,** **we do to you, O Lord.**
Family members together	**Let us pray.** **Dear God,** **We are sorry for the times we have not lived** **according to your laws of love. We will try** **to change our hearts and become more** **like Jesus.**
All	Take time to enjoy a favorite treat or family activity.

I Need to Change My Heart

Sometimes it is hard to be a loving person.
We turn our backs on others. We hurt their feelings. We become selfish and unkind. We find it hard to live according to the Commandments, the Beatitudes, and the Works of Mercy.

We call these hurting actions "sin."

Find the Message about sin by matching the letters with the numbers found below the lines:

A	B	C	D	E	F	G	H	I	J	K	L	M
1	2	3	4	5	6	7	8	9	10	11	12	13

N	O	P	Q	R	S	T	U	V	W	X	Y	Z
14	15	16	17	18	19	20	21	22	23	24	25	26

___ ___ ___ ___   ___ ___   ___ ___ ___,   ___ ___
23 8   5   14   23 5   19 9 14   23 5

___ ___ ___ ___   ___ ___ ___,   " ___   ___ ___   ___ ___ ___ ___ ___ ."
13 21 19 20   19 1 25   9   1 13   19 15 18 18 25

When we sin, we need to change our hearts. We need to reach out to those we have hurt. We also need to forgive those who hurt us.

When we forgive, and when we ask for forgiveness, we become RECONCILED with one another and with God.

In the puzzle below find and circle the words (either running across or up and down) that show ways to become reconciled with others:

hope
comfort
happiness
pardon
peace
forgiveness
love
joy

r	z	j	o	y	i	p	r	f	j
s	f	a	b	l	g	d	y	o	x
k	d	j	c	o	m	f	o	r	t
j	r	h	m	v	x	r	k	g	y
p	e	a	c	e	n	i	l	i	d
c	b	p	r	s	z	e	b	v	n
n	f	p	z	e	t	n	f	e	o
r	t	i	p	a	r	d	o	n	l
l	q	n	w	h	k	s	m	e	k
b	h	e	b	a	l	h	s	s	c
o	x	s	o	r	g	i	y	s	a
v	d	s	h	h	o	p	e	u	d

Here is a picture of me becoming
reconciled with someone I have hurt:

Here is a prayer I can say for
someone I have hurt:

_____

_____

_____

_____

_____

We come to church to celebrate our change of heart.

We come to the priest to ask him to give us God's forgiveness.

We tell the priest what we have done wrong. The priest listens to us and gives us advice. Through the words and actions of the priest, God forgives our sins.

The celebration of forgiveness is called
the Sacrament of Reconciliation.

A sacrament is a special way in which
God touches our lives. Through a sacrament
God's life and love is renewed in us.

When we were baptized, we received the
Sacrament of Baptism.
When we are reconciled with those we
have hurt and ask forgiveness through
the priest, we receive the Sacrament
of Reconciliation.

Dear God,
Thank you for the Sacrament of
Reconciliation. Thank you for your love
and forgiveness. Teach us your ways.

I Receive the Sacrament of Reconciliation

Let

Us

Give

Thanks

and

Praise!

- I take time to think of my sins. How have I turned from God?

- I go to the reconciliation room to talk to the priest.

- The priest helps me to praise God.

- I tell the priest my sins—the things I want to change.

- I say a prayer telling God that I am sorry for my sins and will try to be a more loving person.

- The priest listens to my sins and gives me advice on how to live as God wants me to live.

- The priest asks me to do something to show I really want to change my heart. This is called a "penance." Sometimes the penance is to say certain prayers. Sometimes it is a good action to do for others.

- The priest prays to God for me and says a prayer of forgiveness. Then, he blesses me in "the name of the Father, and of the Son, and of the Holy Spirit."

- My sins are forgiven. God is with me. The priest has helped me turn back to God. I tell the priest, "Thank you!"

listens
blesses
you
priest
praise
penance
sorry
sins

From the list above find the correct word for each sentence below.
Then, match the word to the same sentence number, across or down, in the crossword puzzle:

1. (down) I think of my _____.

2. (across) I talk to the _____.

2. (down) The priest helps me to _____ God.

3. (across) I tell the priest my sins. I tell God I am _____.

4. (across) The priest _____ to my sins.

5. (across) The priest gives me a _____ to do.

6. (down) The priest _____ me. My sins are forgiven.

7. (down) I tell the priest, "Thank _____."

I Turn to God with a Loving Heart

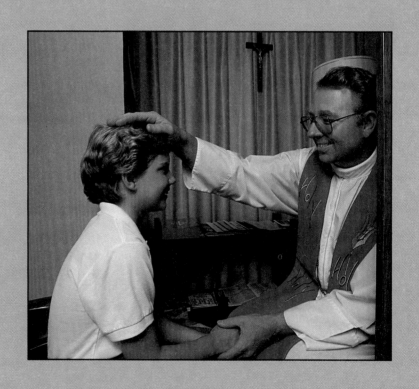

When I turn from God, I sin.
When I do not live according to God's
laws of love, I sin.

Sin hurts me and it hurts others.
I need to change my heart.

Below read the ways that we sometimes sin. Across from each
sinful action, write a way to do something good:

INSTEAD OF . . . I SHOULD . . .

telling a lie _____

_____

cheating in school _____

_____

being selfish _____

_____

staying angry _____

_____

misbehaving in church _____

_____

It is not easy to change our hearts.
We need to ask God to help us.

Each day of our lives we need to forgive
and be forgiven.

We must remember that God does not
want us to sin—but, God *never*
stops loving us.

Here is my prayer thanking God for
love and forgiveness:

_____

_____

_____

_____

_____

_____

_____

The Prodigal Son

Jesus told a story about a boy who changed his heart.

This boy was restless at home. He wanted to get away from his chores, from his father's rules, from his older brother who always seemed to do everything right.

He asked his father to give him his share of the family money. Then, he left home.

The boy did not use his money wisely. He wasted it on things he did not need and on people who said they were his friends just to get some of his money.

One day the boy realized he had nothing left. He had to beg for his food. He had no place to live. Finally, he got a job where he took care of the pigs on a farm. He was so hungry he started to eat some of the food he was feeding the pigs.

He thought about his home, about how he had hurt his father. He realized he had sinned. He knew he had to change his heart. He decided to go back home. He didn't expect to be treated as a son any more, but, he hoped he could at least be a servant in his father's house.

The boy's father had never stopped loving his lost son. He looked down the road for him every day.

It was a wonderful day when he saw his son coming home! He ran to meet him. He threw his arms around him.

The son tried to ask for forgiveness, but the father said, "We will celebrate! We will have a party! My lost son has returned!"

The father invited friends to the party to celebrate his son's change of heart.

Luke 15:11-24

God loves us like the boy's father loved him. Sometimes *we* need to ask for forgiveness as the boy did.

Let us pretend that *you* are the lost boy. You want to receive the Sacrament of Reconciliation. One of your parents can pretend to be the priest.

- First, we need to think of what we did wrong.
  How did the boy sin and turn from God?

_____

_____

_____

- Then, we go to the priest. Together, we praise God through a short prayer. Here is a prayer the boy could say:

_____

_____

_____

- Next, we tell the priest how we have sinned.
  What could the boy say?

_____

_____

_____

- After we tell our sins, we ask God's forgiveness.
  What words could the boy use to ask for forgiveness?

_____

_____

_____

_____

- The priest listens to us and gives us good advice.
  Here is some advice for the lost boy:

_____

_____

_____

_____

- The priest asks us to do something to show we are trying
  to change our hearts. This is called a "penance."
  Here is a penance the priest might give the lost boy:

_____

_____

_____

_____

- Then the priest places his hands on our head and asks
  God to forgive our sins
  **"in the name of the Father
  and of the Son,
  and of the Holy Spirit."**

As he blesses us, we make the Sign of the Cross
in praise of God.

We thank the priest for helping us become reconciled.

This is what the lost boy could say to thank the priest:

_____

_____

_____

_____

70

When we receive the Sacrament of
Reconciliation, we go through the same steps
as we just did with the lost boy
asking for forgiveness.

In the Sacrament of Baptism we were
welcomed into God's family. We receive the
Sacrament of Baptism just one time
in our life.

We may celebrate the Sacrament of
Reconciliation over and over. We may
receive it each time we want to turn
back to God, change our hearts, and ask
for forgiveness.

Family Prayer Time

Family member	**Dear God,** **We thank you for your great love for us.** **We know that each of us needs to change our** **hearts. We need to turn back to you, to ask** **your forgiveness.**
Parent	**Let us listen to the story that Jesus told. The writer** **Luke records this story in the Bible.** Read Luke 15:11-24. **Thank you, God, for this story. It shows how much** **you care for us, your children, even when we sin.** **We are sorry for the times we have sinned.** Each person shares one way he or she would like to change something in his or her life.
Family members (after each sharing)	**"O God, your love can change our hearts."**
Parent	**Soon** _____ **will celebrate** child's name **the Sacrament of Reconciliation for the first time.** **Let us pray for** _____. child's name
Family members	All family members place hands on or over this child. Each person can share his or her own prayer, or all can say together: **Dear God,** **Be with** _____ **as he (she)** child's name **seeks forgiveness through the Sacrament of** **Reconciliation. Give him (her) your peace, your joy.**
All	Close with a favorite song and share a family treat or activity.

Lesson Timetable

Time needed—eight to ten weeks

Lesson 1, Week 1	Classtime for the children	90 minutes
	Input for adults	90 minutes
	Enrollment Ceremony Prayer Service	30 minutes
Lesson 2, Week 2	Child works with parent or care-giver at home	
Lesson 3, Week 3	Same as Lesson 1	
Lesson 4, Week 4	Same as Lesson 2	
Lesson 5, Week 5	Same as Lesson 1	
Lesson 6, Week 6	Same as Lesson 2	
Lesson 7, Week 7	Same as Lesson 1	
Lesson 8, Week 8	Same as Lesson 2	
Week 9 or 10	The Sacrament of Reconciliation	

Suggested times for the lessons:
a) Sunday morning after a parish Eucharistic service
b) Sunday afternoon
c) Early evening on a week night

Lesson 1   I Belong to the Family of God

Classroom lesson with the children and teacher	90 minutes
Enrollment Ceremony Prayer Service with the children, parents, and teachers	30 minutes
Simultaneous session for the adults "The Role of the Parent in Building the Faith Life in the Family"	60 minutes
Preparation for Lesson 2 for use at home with family members	30 minutes
Enrollment Ceremony	30 minutes

Lesson 2   I Live as a Child of God   Lesson Helps for Parent-Teacher (page 79)

Suggestion A	Four sessions at home		
	Session 1 Numbers 1 and 2		30 minutes
	Session 2 Numbers 3 and 4		30 minutes
	Session 3 Numbers 5 and 6		30 minutes
	Session 4 Number 7		30 minutes
Suggestion B	Two sessions at home		
	Session 1 Numbers 1, 2, 3, and 4		60 minutes
	Session 2 Numbers 5, 6, and 7		60 minutes
Suggestion C	One session at home		
	The session may be completed by the parent and child in a school or neighborhood gathering under the direction of the parish's religious education coordinator.		120 minutes

Lesson 3   The Commandments—Numbers 1–5

Classroom lesson with the children and teacher	90 minutes
Prayer service with parents and children	30 minutes
Simultaneous session with adults "The Ten Commandments Today"	60 minutes
Preparation for Lesson 4 for use at home with family members	30 minutes

73

Lesson 4 The Commandments—Numbers 6–10 Lesson Helps for Parent-Teacher (page 81)

	Suggestion A	Four sessions at home	
		Session 1 Numbers 1, 2, and 3	**30 minutes**
		Session 2 Numbers 4, 5, and 6	**30 minutes**
		Session 3 Numbers 7, 8	**30 minutes**
		Session 4 Number 9—Prayer time with other family members	**30 minutes**
	Suggestion B	Two sessions at home	
		Session 1 Numbers 1, 2, 3, 4, 5, and 6	**60 minutes**
		Session 2 Numbers 7, 8, and 9	**60 minutes**
	Suggestion C	One session at home	
		The session may be completed by the parent and child in a school or neighborhood gathering under the direction of the parish's religious education coordinator.	**120 minutes**

Lesson 5 The Beatitudes: "Happy are they . . ."

Classroom lesson with the children and teacher	**90 minutes**
Prayer service with parents and children	**30 minutes**
Simultaneous session with adults	
"The Beatitudes and Works of Mercy"	**60 minutes**
Preparation for Lesson 6 for use at home with family members	**30 minutes**

Lesson 6 The Works of Mercy: We Serve One Another Lesson Helps for Parent-Teacher (page 84)

	Suggestion A	Three sessions at home	
		Session 1 Numbers 1, 2, 3, and 4	**30 minutes**
		Session 2 Numbers 5, 6, and 7	**30 minutes**
		Session 3 Number 8—Prayer time with family members	**30 minutes**
	Suggestion B	Two sessions at home	
		Session 1 Numbers 1, 2, 3, 4, and 5	**60 minutes**
		Session 2 Numbers 7 and 8	**45–60 minutes**
	Suggestion C	One session at home	
		The session may be completed by parent and child in a school or neighborhood gathering under the direction of the parish's religious education coordinator.	**120 minutes**

Lesson 7 I Need to Change My Heart

Classroom lesson with the children and teacher	**30 minutes**
Prayer service with children and parents	**30 minutes**
Simultaneous session with adults	
"The Rite of Reconciliation"	**60 minutes**
Preparation for Lesson 8 for use at home with family members	
Prayer service with children and parents	**30 minutes**

Lesson 8 I Turn to God with a Loving Heart Lesson Helps for Parent-Teacher (page 86)

	Suggestion A	Three sessions at home	
		Session 1 Numbers 1, 2, and 3	**30 minutes**
		Session 2 Numbers 4, 5, and 6	**30 minutes**
		Session 3 Numbers 7 and 8	**30 minutes**
	Suggestion B	Two sessions at home	
		Session 1 Numbers 1, 2, 3, 4, and 5	**60 minutes**
		Session 2 Numbers 6, 7, and 8	**45 minutes**
	Suggestion C	One session at home	
		The session may be completed by parent and child in a school or neighborhood gathering under the direction of the parish's religious education coordinator.	**120 minutes**

Lesson Objectives and Materials

Lesson 1   I Belong to the Family of God

Objectives:
1. The child realizes that he or she is a good person with special talents to share with others. The child can rejoice in the gift of life.
2. The child understands that he or she is special to God and to the people of God, especially his or her family.
3. The child helps compose a prayer asking God to help him or her grow in goodness.
4. The child enrolls in the parish's Reconciliation Program.

Classroom Materials: This book, name tags, colors, pencils

Enrollment Ceremony Materials: Enrollment Badges, this book, pen or pencil, favorite music selections of praise and love

Parent Preparation Materials: Nametags, filmstrip, video, movie, or booklet on faith (*see* page 87, session 1, number 1), paper, pencils for small group discussions

Lesson 2   I Live as a Child of God

Objectives:
1. The child hears the story of his or her own baptism.
2. The child is introduced to the Church as family and discusses ways to show love to the members of this family.
3. Family members spend time affirming the goodness of one another and recognize times when they have not shown enough love.
4. The family celebrates love and forgiveness through shared prayer.

Materials: This book, pictures, and other memorabilia from the child's baptism, markers for the game on page 13, colors, pencils, one candle per person for the prayer service, Bible, candle, plant, etc., to provide a special place for the family's sharing

Lesson 3   The Commandments—Numbers 1–5

Objectives:
1. The child is introduced to the first five Commandments.
2. The child begins to understand how these Commandments can help him or her become a more loving person.
3. The child learns how a change of heart can take place by discussing the Scripture reading about Zacchaeus.
4. Parents and child take part in the Commandment Badge Prayer Service.

Classroom Materials: This book, nametags, colors, pencils, magazine pictures showing love and caring, glue, scissors, Bible (Luke 19:1-9)

Commandment Badge Service Materials: Commandment Badges, favorite music selection, Bible reading . . . the story of Zacchaeus

Parent Preparation Materials: Nametags, filmstrip, video, etc. (*see* page 87, session 2, number 1), copy of the Ten Commandments (*see* page 88), pencils, paper

Lesson 4   The Commandments—Numbers 6–10

Objectives:
1. The child is introduced to Commandments 6–10.
2. The child begins to understand how these Commandments can help him or her become a more loving person.
3. The family celebrates love and forgiveness through a time of shared prayer.

Materials: This book, colors, pencils, Bible, candle, plant, etc., to provide a special place for family sharing

Lesson 5   The Beatitudes: "Happy are they . . ."

Objectives:	1. The child is introduced to the Beatitudes.
	2. The child discusses how living the Beatitudes can help him or her to grow in love.
	3. Parent and child take part in the Beatitude Badge Prayer Service.
Classroom Materials:	This book, nametags, colors, pencils
Beatitude Badge Service Materials:	Beatitude Badges, favorite music selections
Parent Preparation Materials:	Nametags, filmstrip, video, etc. (*see* page 87, session 3, number 1) copy of the Beatitudes and Works of Mercy (*see* page 86), paper, pencils

Lesson 6   The Works of Mercy: We Serve One Another

Objectives:	1. The child is introduced to the corporal Works of Mercy.
	2. The child discusses how living the Works of Mercy can help him or her to reach out to others in kindness and compassion.
	3. The child is introduced to the concept of being thankful to God for the many blessings in his or her own life.
	4. The family celebrates kindness and forgiveness through a time of shared prayer.
Materials Needed:	This book, newspapers or magazine pictures of needy people, Bible for Scripture passages (*see* list on page 53) and for prayer service, colors, pencils, Bible, candle, plant, etc., to provide a special place for family sharing

Lesson 7   I Need to Change My Heart

Objectives:	1. The child discusses how sin turns him or her away from God and from others and how reconciliation can take place through forgiveness.
	2. The child is introduced to the Rite of Reconciliation.
	3. Parents and child take part in a prayer service on brokenness and change of heart.
Classroom Materials:	This book, nametags, colors, pencils
Turn Away from Sin Badge Service Materials:	Large heart, small hearts listing the short phrases on page 85, the Turn Away from Sin Badges, tape or glue
Parent Preparation Materials:	Nametags, filmstrip, video, etc. (*see* page 88, session 4, number 1), paper and pencils for small group discussions

Lesson 8   I Turn to God with a Loving Heart

Objectives:	1. The child deepens his or her understanding of the Sacrament of Reconciliation as he or she reviews what this sacrament means.
	2. The child discusses how the story of the Prodigal Son (Luke 15:11-24) teaches love, forgiveness, and reconciliation.
	3. The parent and child role-play the Rite of Reconciliation using the characters from the story of the Prodigal Son.
	4. The family celebrates a change of heart through a time of shared prayer.
Materials:	This book, pencils, colors, Bible for story of the Prodigal Son, cards for inviting relatives and friends to the child's first reconciliation service

Lesson Helps*

Lesson 1   I Belong to the Family of God

FOR TEACHER AND CLASS

1. Gather the children and give them a warm welcome.
   - Introduce yourself and mention some activity that you enjoy.
   - Ask each child to tell the class his or her name and something that he or she likes to do (a sport, reading, playing with a family pet, visiting someone special, etc.).

2. Tell the children that God has given the gift of life to all of our world.
   - Trees, flowers, animals, and birds are all alive, but they do not know that they have life. They can't be happy that they are alive. Only PEOPLE can be happy to be alive.
   - Ask what we can do because we are ALIVE.
   - Open this book to page 1. Ask the children how they can tell that the boy in this picture is *glad* to be alive.
   - Ask the children to pray with you the prayer on this page: "Thank you, God, for the gift of life."

3. Turn to page 2 of this book. Read "Here is an announcement about my birth."
   - Ask the children to share how the announcement of their birth might have been written in the daily newspaper. Then, have each child write an announcement of his or her birth in the NEWS! NEWS! NEWS! section of page 2.

4. Ask the children to think of people who were happy to know about their birth—parents, grandparents, brothers, sisters, aunts, uncles, cousins, and friends.
   - Read "Many people were glad I was born" and have the children fill in the blanks.

5. Tell the children that every person God made is a GOOD person. Sometimes people do *bad things*, but that doesn't make them *bad persons*. Every person IS SPECIAL. We each have gifts that we can use to be good persons. We call these gifts TALENTS.
   - Ask the children to share about a talent they know they have.
   - Then, tell them that there are some talents that all of us can learn to share with others. We can be . . . friendly . . . gentle . . . cheerful . . . truthful . . . kind, etc.
   - Have the children pray with you the prayer on page 3: "Thank you, God, for the talents that you have given to me."

6. Turn to page 4 and the list of words in the "Talent Search."
   - Read through this list of talents.
   - Do the puzzle together.

7. Turn to and read page 5.
   - Remind the children that you have already said that EACH person is special. FAMILIES are special too.
   - Ask what families can do to show love for one another.

8. Read page 6 and have the children fill in the blanks.
   - Show the children how to work through the word puzzle.

9. Ask the children how many of them have seen a baby baptized.
   - Ask them why they think the family takes the baby to church to be baptized.
   - Together read the sentence on the top half of page 7.

10. Look at the sentences on the bottom of page 7.
    - Have the children put the correct words in these sentences.
    - Let them fill in the crossword puzzle with the same words.

11. As you close the lesson today, have the children read the message on page 8.
    - Ask them to write a prayer to God—or compose this prayer as a class.

*These suggestions and directives are either for the teacher to use in the classroom or for the parent-teacher to use at home while working with the child.

ENROLLMENT CEREMONY

Bring the parents and children together in the parish church or in a room set up for a prayerful celebration.

Invite the pastor, an associate pastor or deacon, the religious education coordinator, or a teacher to lead the Enrollment Ceremony. Other leaders may participate in the signing part of this service.

All   Begin with a simple song of praise, familiar to the children and parents.

Leader   **Today we welcome all of you boys and girls and all of you parents to this prayer service. You have come to prepare to receive a special sacrament in the Catholic Church. It is called Recon-**

77

ciliation. Reconciliation is a big word that means *forgiving and loving one another.*

Each lesson in the book you are using will prepare you to receive this beautiful sacrament. It will help you celebrate forgiveness.

Boys and girls, as you use "Reconciliation—A Change of Heart," you will learn how important it is to have a loving and forgiving heart.

As you come forward today, bring along your parents and your book. I will ask each child, "Do you wish to prepare for the Sacrament of Reconciliation by being a loving and forgiving child?"

If you choose to answer YES, we will give you an Enrollment Badge and ask you to sign your name on the inside cover of your book.

Then, I will ask each parent, "Will you help your child prepare for the Sacrament of Reconciliation by trying to be a loving and forgiving parent?" When you answer YES, you can also sign your child's book.

During the time of commitment and signing, music could be playing softly in the background.

When each child has been enrolled, ask everyone to pray with you by responding "Thank you for your gifts, Lord."

Leader	**Dear Lord, we are happy to be alive.**
All	**Thank you for your gifts, Lord.**
Leader	**Dear Lord, we thank you for our talents.**
All	**Thank you for your gifts, Lord.**
Leader	**Dear Lord, we thank you for loving families and friends.**
All	**Thank you for your gifts, Lord.**
Leader	**Dear Lord, we thank you for the Sacrament of Reconciliation.**
All	**Thank you for your gifts, Lord.**
All	Close with a song having words of love and forgiveness.

Lesson 2   I Live as a Child of God

FOR PARENTS AND CHILD

Find a special place in the home to use this lesson. A candle for each family member and a Bible for all to refer to should be available.

1. Open this book to pages 9 and 10 and talk about your child's baptism.
   - Photographs of the baptism may be useful during the lesson.
   - Tell your child why you wanted to have him or her baptized.
   - Tell your child the name of the church and the name of the priest who baptized him or her.
   - Tell your child why you chose his or her name.
   - Read: "The priest or the deacon prayed _____" and have your child put his or her name on the line after the words "I baptize you _____."
   - Go on to page 11.

2. Let your child put a favorite baptism photo at the top of page 11 or have him or her draw a picture of the baptism.
   - Help your child fill in the bottom of the page: "My godparents are _____" and "Many people came to celebrate my baptism. Their names are _____."

3. Turn to and read page 12.
   - Ask your child how he or she might bring God's love to your family, to your neighborhood, to friends.
   - Talk about how the people in the picture on this page are bringing God's love to others.
   - Then, pray together the prayer on this page.

4. Look at the game on page 13. You can decide to use it during this lesson—or at another time.
   - Whether you play the game or not, read the blocks with the various behaviors and ask your child to find the ones where people are sharing God's life and love with others.

5. Turn to page 14 and talk about the pictures.
   - Discuss with your child how it feels when we know we hurt someone—or when we are hurt by family members or friends.
   - Ask what might have happened to bring happiness to the people in the picture at the bottom of the page.
   - The child should read the sentences at the top of the page.
   - Then, read together the prayer on this page.

6. Your child can complete page 15 now or at a later time.
   - Take time to find the loving actions amid the hurting ones.

7. Turn to page 16. This is a *family* prayer time.
   - Use it at a time when as many members of your family as possible can be together. You will need one candle per person if possible.
   - After one parent reads the opening prayer, each family member may share one way he or she has shown love. Perhaps the parents can begin this sharing (for example, "I gave each of you a hug today"; "I made your favorite dessert on Thursday"; "I read a story to Mary"; "I went to John's basketball game," etc.). The children may choose one of many ways in which they shared love at home or school.
   - After each person lights a candle, all of the family members say, "Let us give thanks to God."

- It is important for children to know that everyone fails to love at times—even parents. For example, a parent may offer, "I was upset at work and said hurtful things about someone in the office"; "I was in a hurry today and didn't take time to listen to Mr. Jones when he needed to talk to me"; "I did not show respect for God's name when I was angry today."
- Then your children may share. Help them only if they cannot think of a way they were unloving.
- No judgments are made at all. Each person says, "I'm sorry," and blows out his or her candle to show how unloving actions can take the joy and light out of someone's life. The family responds, "We ask your forgiveness, Lord."
- The family prays together the prayer, and the candles are relit. A parent then invites everyone to join in the Our Father.
- Close with a favorite song to celebrate love and forgiveness.
- Celebrate love and forgiveness with some type of family treat.

Lesson 3   The Commandments—Numbers 1–5

FOR TEACHER AND CLASS

1. Gather the children and welcome them back to class.

2. Ask the children to tell you some rules they are to follow at home or in school.
   - Ask them what could happen if no one followed any rules.
   - Ask how rules can *help* us.

3. Open this book to pages 17 and 18.
   - Discuss how the family is keeping some rules as they work together.
   - Read the top of page 18. Then, the children may do the bottom section individually, or together as a class.

4. God's family needs rules, too, to help people love and care for each other.
   - Read carefully the "Ten Commandments" on page 19.

5. Read the top of page 20 and look at the pictures.
   - When do people make things more important than God?
   - Pray together the prayer on page 20.

6. Look at the words in the photo on page 21.
   - What name of God is used?
   - How can we tell it is being used without love and respect?
   - Pray together the prayer on this page.

7. Let the children complete page 22.
   - Read together the names for God.
   - Have the children find the correct places for them and have them find the Commandment message.

8. Read together the Third Commandment on page 23.
   - Tell the children that going to church is one important way of keeping God first in our lives.
   - On page 23 read the ways we can use to keep Sunday as God's day.

9. On page 24 have the children find their way to church through the maze.

10. On page 25, read the Fourth Commandment and the explanation of it.
    - Ask the children how parents can love us into goodness.
    - Ask why they think parents need our prayers.
    - Pray together the prayer on this page.

11. Read the Fifth Commandment and the sentences on page 26.
    - Ask how we treat others when we are angry.
    - Ask how we treat others when we are afraid.
    - How can we be nice to people we don't even like.
    - Pray together the prayer on this page.

12. On page 27 have the children draw or paste magazine clippings of people treating each other with love and respect.

13. Introduce the children to the story about Zacchaeus, who lived when Jesus did.
    Sample introduction:
    Jesus was always loving and kind and he thought of the needs of other people. He treated everyone with respect. Zacchaeus was not so good. He was not honest. He thought money was more important than God. The people in his town did not like him. One day Zacchaeus met Jesus. Jesus showed Zacchaeus kindness and love and Zacchaeus changed his heart. He became loving, kind, and generous. He gave most of his money away.
    - Read the story of Zacchaeus from Luke 19:1-10 or from memory tell your account of Zacchaeus' change of heart.
    - Read together the prayer on page 28.

COMMANDMENT BADGE PRAYER SERVICE

All	Sing an opening song.
Leader	Reads story of Zacchaeus from Luke 19:1-10.
Leader	**Zacchaeus met Jesus and became a new, loving person. He changed his life.**
	Let us ask God to help us change our own lives.
	We have been selfish.
All	**Help us to change our lives.**
Leader	**We have hurt the feelings of others.**
All	**Help us to change our lives.**
Leader	**We have not made God's Day an important day each week.**
All	**Help us to change our lives.**
Leader	**We have not shown respect to our parents, grandparents, and teachers.**
All	**Help us to change our lives.**
Leader	**We have been lazy and did not help at home.**
All	**Help us to change our lives.**
Leader	**We have stayed angry at those who have hurt us.**
All	**Help us to change our lives.**

Leader	God's laws help us to love God, ourselves, and others. Today, you will come forward to receive your Commandment Badge. I (or another of the leaders) will ask each of you to read your badge as it is handed to you.

After the badges have been handed out, the leader prays:

Leader	Happy are those who are good, who walk in the way of our God. Happy are those who keep God's laws, who seek God with all their heart.

All	Sing "This Is My Commandment," "Hi! God," or some other song.

Lesson 4 The Commandments—Numbers 6–10

FOR PARENTS AND CHILD

Arrange a special place again in your home, using a Bible, a plant, perhaps a statue, a picture, and other items that remind us of God's Presence.

1. Read page 30 with your child.
   - Ask your child what he or she thinks being "faithful" means.
   - Tell the child that in a marriage a husband and wife are to love one another for their lifetime.
   - Sometimes, however, a divorce takes place because the love between husband and wife does not grow. The couple becomes so unhappy that they decide not to live together.
   - A divorce is very hard for everyone in a family. Each person hurts inside. The husband and wife worry about the children. Even though they cannot stay together as a family, they still love the children.
   - If parents or relatives become divorced, it is important for children to let them know that they still love them.
   - The Sixth Commandment also asks us to respect our bodies and the bodies of others. We each have the wonderful gift of life. Through this body new life is given to children. We are not to make fun of our own body or the bodies of others.
   - If we have this respect for ourselves and others, it will be easier to keep the promise to be faithful in our love in marriage.

2. Continue on page 30.
   - Have your child circle the words that will help him or her be a faithful friend.
   - Ask your child to read the scrambled words and put together a sentence about a faithful friend.

3. Read page 31 with your child.
   - Ask your child what kinds of things people steal.
   - Why is stealing wrong?
   - How can we make up for what is taken from others?
   - Pray together the prayer on the page.

4. Go on to the maze on page 32.
   - Have your child find the path that will help the boy take what he stole back to the store.

5. Read page 33 to introduce the Eighth Commandment.
   - Ask your child when they think people lie.
   - Ask why they think people decide to lie.
   - Ask why it is hard to tell the truth sometimes.
   - How can lies hurt other people?
   - Perhaps you can tell the story of the boy who cried "wolf" too many times.
   - Read together the prayer on this page.

6. Have your child follow the directions on page 34 (to find the word "honest").

7. On page 35 read the Ninth and Tenth Commandments.
   - Help your child understand that WANTING something that belongs to another person isn't wrong. PLANNING to take it away, even if the plan doesn't work, is what is wrong.
   - Ask your child what kind of things people might plan to take away from someone (e.g., bike, car, money, pets, jewelry, even another person).
   - Read together the prayer on this page.

8. Page 36 reviews the Ten Commandments.
   - Help your child answer the true-false statements.
   - Help them identify each Commandment statement on the bottom half of this page with the correct Commandment number.

9. Turn to page 37 for the Family Prayer Time.
   - Gather as many of your family as possible for this sharing.
   - The opening prayer is read by anyone chosen by the family. Then, sharing is done in the same way as Lesson 2.
   - Each family member shares at least one way he or she has shown love and goodness during the past day or two.
   - Family members respond, *"Thank you for the gift of love."*
   - Each person shares one way he or she did not share enough love. The other family members respond, *"We are sorry, Lord."*
   - When each has had time to share, turn to the heart on page 38. Complete this as a family. When this is finished, pray together the prayer on this page.
   - Celebrate with a specially planned treat or outing.

Lesson 5 The Beatitudes:
"Happy are they . . ."

FOR TEACHER AND CLASS

1. Gather the children and have them turn to page 39.
   - As they look at the picture, ask them to tell you why each person is happy.

2. Turn to page 40 and read the first paragraph.
   - Tell the children that Jesus gave us a special list of things that we can do to be happy. We call this list the "Beatitudes." The word means that God will bless us as we do things for others.
   - Read through the Beatitudes together. Then stress the last paragraph—our reward for living the Beatitudes is to be with God in the Kingdom of Heaven.

3. Read the heading on page 41. Work through page 41 in teams or individually. Have the children read each box.
   - Whenever they find something God would want us to do, have them outline those boxes with a favorite color.
   - The poor in spirit always place God first in their lives. They depend on God.

4. Read the Beatitude verse together on page 42.
   - How do we know when someone is gentle?
   - How was Jesus gentle?
   - Have the children fill in one word next to each letter of the word "gentle." The word should start with the same letter (G—"grateful," "gracious," etc.). They may use the words at the bottom of this page or words of their choosing.

5. Read the Beatitude verse together on page 43.
   - How do we mourn for someone?
   - This Beatitude tells us that it is all right to show our sad feelings.
   - When we mourn we can learn to help others who are sad. We can tell them we do understand.
   - We can learn that God loves us even in our sad, lonely times. God helps us to find peace in our hearts.
   - Look at the flowers on this page. Read the words around each flower. Which ones name people or things that can help us find comfort and peace when we mourn?

- Outline these flowers with a favorite color. The correct flowers (friends, priest, parents, prayer, doctor) will spell JESUS in the center circles.

6. Read together the Beatitude on page 44.
   - When we say we "hunger and thirst" for what is right, we mean that doing what is right is just as important to us as our food and drink.
   - What in our world today needs to be made right?
   - When might we make things right in our schools? (Are people cheating? are they kind? are they showing respect?, etc.)
   - When might we make things right in our homes? (Are we honest? are we showing love? are we praying together?, etc.)
   - Have the children complete the mystery puzzle on this page.

7. Read together the Beatitude on page 45.
   - What do we mean when we say, "Have mercy on me."?
   - How can we show mercy and forgiveness?
   - Why is it hard sometimes to show mercy?
   - Have the children do the dot-to-dot exercise on this page.

8. Read together the Beatitude on page 46 and the sentences by the picture.
   - How do we know the persons in this picture are happy?
   - It is important to know that God loves each of us. He sees the good in each person.
   - Have the children write some good things about themselves at the bottom of this page.

9. Read the Beatitude on page 47.
   - When do we need to be peacemakers?
   - Do you know of any grown-ups who are peacemakers?
   - Why do we need peacemakers in our homes, our schools, our towns, our world?
   - Have the children draw a picture showing one way they might bring peace to someone.

10. Read the Eighth Beatitude on page 48.
    - Doing the right thing sometimes makes us suffer. People make fun of us. Sometimes they hurt us. That is what happened to Jesus. He had to suffer because he was doing the right things each day of his life.
    - Have the children write on the cross one way that they suffer and carry their own crosses.

PRAYER CELEBRATION

All	Sing a familiar song.
Leader	**Dear God,** **Help us to put you first in our lives. Help us to depend on you instead of ourselves.**
All	**Help us to be poor in spirit.**

Leader	**Dear God,**
	Help us to reach out to others with kindness, love, and respect.
All	**Help us to be gentle.**
Leader	**Dear God,**
	Help us to show our feelings when we are sad. Let the deaths of loved ones make us better persons who can understand the heartaches of other people.
All	**Help us to mourn.**
Leader	**Dear God,**
	Help us to do everything we can to make things right in our world. Teach us to be honest, helpful, and caring.
All	**Help us to hunger and thirst for what is right.**
Leader	**Dear God,**
	Help us to forgive others when they hurt us. Instead of trying to get even, teach us to forgive as Jesus did.
All	**Help us to be merciful.**
Leader	**Dear God,**
	Help us to see how good we really are. You know our hearts and see our desire to live as you want us to live.
All	**Help us to be pure in heart.**
Leader	**Dear God,**
	Help us to take the first steps in bringing about peace at home, at school, at work, wherever we go.
All	**Help us to be peacemakers.**
Leader	**Dear God,**
	Help us to know that sometimes we must suffer because we have done something good. Instead of becoming angry, help us to carry our crosses, just as Jesus carried his. We know the cross will lead us to you.
All	**Help us to suffer for doing what is right.**
Leader	**Today, each child will receive a Beatitude Badge. Would the parents come forward with your child. Please place your hands on your child during the prayer:**

Large groups may use several leaders for this prayer.

Lesson 6   The Works of Mercy: We Serve One Another

FOR PARENTS AND CHILD

Arrange a special place for this session. Use your Bible, a plant, statue, picture, etc. to remind everyone of God's Presence.

1. Read page 50 with your child.
   - The Church calls this list of activities the "Corporal Works of Mercy." They are ways we remember the needy and reach out to them.

2. Read the story on page 51 about the loaves and fishes.

3. Read page 52 and help your child find clippings from newspapers and magazines of people in need.
   - Talk about why these people need help and love.
   - Are there poor people in your city, in your neighborhood?
   - How can you touch their lives?

4. Read the passage from Luke on page 53.
   - Ask your child to answer *yes* or *no* to the phrases that may or may not show selfishness.

5. Use a Bible for the lesson on the bottom half of page 53. Read each Gospel passage in Column A with your child and, together, match the messages in Column B that correspond with the readings.

6. On page 54 read the story about the ten lepers.
   - How would you feel if people forgot to thank you for the good things you do?
   - Do we need a thank you for all of the good things we do?
   - Who are people that we sometimes forget to thank?

7. On page 55 have your child decode the message on the wheel starting with "V" and putting every other letter, working clockwise, on the lines below the wheel.
   - The message is: "Visit the Sick, Help the Poor."

8. Gather as many family members as possible for the family prayer on page 56.
   - Any family member can read the opening prayer.
   - Another family member can read the verses from the Gospel of Matthew (25:31-40).
   - Then each member of the family shares one way he or she has shown love and kindness to another person.
   - After each person shares the good thing he or she has done, everyone can respond: "Whatever we do to others, we do to you, O Lord."
   - Then each member of the family shares one way he or she has hurt someone through word, action, neglect, etc.
   - When each finishes, the family members can again respond: "Whatever we do to others, we do to you, O Lord."

- When the sharing is finished, pray together this prayer:

Dear God,

We are sorry for the times we have not lived according to your laws of love. We will try to change our hearts and become more like Jesus.

- Celebrate with a favorite treat or family activity.

Lesson 7   I Need to Change My Heart

FOR TEACHER AND CLASS

1. Gather the children and turn to page 57.
   - Read the title and discuss how the picture shows ways of loving and forgiving.

2. Read page 58 and ask the children: "Can you think of some ways in which we sin?"
   - When we sin, we hurt ourselves and others. We turn away from God. We need to say, "I am sorry."
   - Have the children decode the message on this page: "When we sin, we must say, 'I am sorry.'"

3. Read page 59 and explain that "reconciled" means that we heal a hurt relationship. We change our ways. We forgive others. We receive forgiveness from those we have hurt.
   - Have the children do the "search a word."
   - Find: peace   happiness   joy   love
     comfort   hope   pardon   forgiveness

4. Ask the children to draw a sketch of themselves on page 60 showing how they have "turned back" to a family member or friend they have hurt.
   - Each child can write a prayer for someone he or she has hurt or do this together as a class.

5. Read page 61 and ask the children: "What kind of advice could the priest give if someone said he or she told lies, disobeyed parents and teachers, shoplifted from stores, etc.?"

6. Read page 62 and tell the children that the Church celebrates seven sacraments, one of which they have already received—baptism.
   - Soon they will receive the Sacrament of Reconciliation. (Some perhaps have also received the Sacrament of the Eucharist.)
   - In each sacrament God comes into our lives in a special way.
   - Pray together the prayer on this page.

7. Read page 63 on how to receive the Sacrament of Reconciliation.
   - Take time to role-play the reception of this sacrament.

8. On page 64 work through the crossword puzzle which reviews the steps in the Rite of Reconciliation.
   - You may wish to have the children do this together.

9. Gather the parents and children together for prayer.

Leader

Dear God,

We are sorry for the hurt and brokenness we have caused
in our family (pause) **and**
with our friends. (pause)
We want to change our hearts,
to heal the brokenness around us.
We want to be people

- **who love**
- **of peace**
- **of joy**
- **of hope**
- **of kindness**
- **of courage**
- **who share**
- **who forgive**
- **who pray**
- **who listen**
- **who are truthful**
- **who are honest**
- **who are thoughtful**
- **who are helpful**

Make a large heart with a jagged line to show brokenness.

Make small cards or hearts with the list of words telling what kind of people we want to be. You may need to make more than one of each.

Have each child draw out a heart (or paper) from a container. When the leader reads the list of words, the child with that word comes forward to paste it or to tape it on the broken heart.

Reader

Let us listen to the words of Jesus from the Gospel of John:

"Peace is my gift to you . . . .
Peace is my farewell to you,
My peace is my gift to you;
Do not be distressed or fearful.
. . . in me you can find peace.
You will suffer in the world,
But take courage!
I have overcome the world.
The commandment I give you is this,
That you love one another.

John 14–15

Leader

We find peace of heart and love for one another when we turn
from sin.
Our badge today is "Turn from Sin." Turn back to God with a
loving heart.
Come forward now to receive your badge.

_____ (name) **Turn from sin.**
Turn back to God with a loving heart.
I will.

When the children have received their badges,
close with a favorite song.

Lesson 8 I Turn to God with a Loving Heart

FOR PARENT AND CHILD

Arrange a special place for this last session. Use a Bible, plant, statue, picture, etc. to remind everyone of God's Presence.

1. On page 65 read the title of the lesson with your child.
   - Take a few minutes to review the meaning of the word "reconciliation."
   - How does the picture on this page show reconciliation?

2. Read through page 66.
   - Help your child complete the exercise on this page.

3. Read page 67 together.
   - Ask your child to compose a prayer to God.

4. Page 68 tells the story of the Prodigal Son.
   - Read through this story together. Then ask your child:
   - Why did the boy leave his home?
   - Why did he return home?
   - Why do you think the father wanted to celebrate the boy's return?

5. Turn to page 69. These next pages take your child through the steps that take place during the Sacrament of Reconciliation.
   - You can do this by role-playing the story of the Prodigal Son. Your child can be the lost son and you can be the priest. As you read through each step, help your child to fill in the blanks on pages 69–70.

6. Conclude this role-playing time by reading the message on page 71.
   - Explain that once someone has received the Sacrament of Reconciliation, it can be received as often as one wishes to ask forgiveness.
   - It would be helpful for your child to see you, as adults, receiving the sacrament. It is important for children to see that adults also recognize the need to change their heart and celebrate forgiveness.

7. As you finish this lesson on page 72, bring your entire family together for prayer.
   - From the Bible read the story of the Prodigal Son (Luke 15:11-24).
   - Continue with ways each family member would like to change his or her heart.
   - The family members, then, pray for and bless the child preparing to celebrate the Sacrament of Reconciliation for the first time.

8. After the closing prayer, the family may take time to share a treat or a special activity.
   - This time could also be used to make invitations for grandparents, godparents, etc. to attend the child's first celebration of this sacrament.

SAMPLE PRAYERS OF CONTRITION

Dear God,
I am sorry for the times I have turned from you.
I ask forgiveness.
Help me to be a loving child.
Help me to grow in goodness.
I love you. I praise you.
I thank you for your love.

Dear God,
I know that I have not lived according to your laws of love.
Forgive me for the times I have turned away from you.
I have turned away from the people you have asked me to love.
Help me to change my heart.
Give me your peace.

Dear God,
I love you above all things.
Forgive me for the times I have not loved enough.
I am sorry for my sins.
Help me to reach out to your people in kindness and love.

BEATITUDES

Happy are the poor in spirit.
Happy are the gentle.
Happy are those who mourn.
Happy are those who hunger and thirst for what is right.
Happy are the merciful.
Happy are the pure in heart.
Happy are the peacemakers.
Happy are those who suffer as they protect and defend what is right.

WORKS OF MERCY

Feed the hungry.
Give drink to the thirsty.
Clothe the naked.
Visit the sick.
Visit those in prison.
Shelter those without a home.
Bury those who die.

Parent Preparation*

The Role of the Parent in Building the Faith Life in the Family

SESSION 1 (120 minutes)

1. Welcome the parents and begin with a talk on faith life in the family or with one of the Suggested Resources (20–30 minutes):

   Suggested Resources:

   God and Your Children, a 23-minute film or videotape. Available for sale or rental from Teleketics, Franciscan Communications, 1229 S. Santee St., Los Angeles, CA 90015.

   Light and Salt: The Challenge of Faith by Joanne McPortland. A 32-page booklet available, with discount on large quantities, from Franciscan Communications, 1229 S. Santee St., Los Angeles, CA 90015.

   Faith from *The Search for God,* a series of five 30-minute segments by John Powell, S.J. Available from Argus Communications, P.O. Box 7000, One DLM Park, Allen, TX 75002.

2. Divide the parents into discussion groups of 6–10 people.
   - Use the discussion questions (see number 3) in these small groups.
   - Use an average of ten minutes per question.
   - Then, come together as a large group and share the answers given by each small group (about 20 minutes).

3. **Discussion Questions:**
   - How can parents share their faith-life with their children?
   - Why do we hear today that parents are the primary teachers of religion?
   - How can we, as parents, find ways to update and grow in our faith life?

4. Explain to the parents that the next lesson on the Sacrament of Reconciliation should be done at home. It centers on baptism and faith.
   - Lesson 2 is especially for parent-and-child sharing. Go through this lesson with the parents (20–30 minutes).
   - Stress the importance of the "Family Prayer Time" at the end of the lesson for *all* family members. It is a time of prayer and celebration for the entire family.

5. Bring the parents and children together for the Enrollment Ceremony.

The Ten Commandments Today

SESSION 2 (120 minutes)

1. Welcome the parents and begin with a talk on the Commandments or with one of the Suggested Resources (20–30 minutes):

   Suggested Resources:

   Commandments: Alternatives for Community Life, script by Brian A. Haggerty, filmstrip with guidebook and cassette. Available from Paulist Press, 997 MacArthur Blvd., Mahwah, NJ 07430.

   Moral Values, a filmstrip with cassette and study guide. Ikonographics filmstrip available from The Winston-Seabury Press. Phone the toll-free number 1-800-328-5125.

   The Commandments, a filmstrip with studyguide and cassette. Ikonographics filmstrip available from The Winston-Seabury Press. Phone the toll-free number 1-800-328-5125.

   - Hand out a copy of page 88.† Explain that the wording of the Commandments has been simplified to make the Commandments understandable to children.

2. Divide into small groups of six to ten people as in Session 1 (see Number 2 from Session 1).

3. **Discussion Questions:**
   - Do you think it is important to let your child know that you find it as difficult to keep the Commandments as they do?
   - In the past we have considered the Commandments as rigid rules to be observed. Today we stress they are "laws of love" to bring us closer to God and to one another. How can this shift in emphasis bring about a better attitude toward the Commandments?
   - What are some effective ways of helping your child follow these laws of love?

4. Lesson 4 on the Ten Commandments (see pages 29–38) is the parent-child lesson to be done at home.
   - Go through this lesson with the parents (20–30 minutes). Stress again the importance of the "Family Prayer Time."

5. Bring the parents and children together for the Commandment Badge Prayer Service.
   - Hand out copies of page 86 on the Beatitudes and the Works of Mercy.† Explain that the Commandments are only part of the way we are to live and grow in our faith. Jesus gave us the Beatitudes and Works of Mercy to help give direction to the way we love God and our neighbor.

†The Liturgical Press grants permission to duplicate this page for this purpose.

The Beatitudes and Works of Mercy

SESSION 3 (120 minutes)

1. Welcome the parents and begin with a talk on the Beatitudes and the Works of Mercy or with one of the Suggested Resources (20–30 minutes):

   Suggested Resources:

   The Challenge of the Beatitudes, a filmstrip available from ROA, 6633 W. Howard St., Niles, IL 60648.

   The Beatitudes, a filmstrip with cassette and study guide. Ikonographics filmstrips available from The Winston-Seabury Press. Phone the toll-free number 1-800-328-5125.

   They Shall See, a 17-minute film or video. Available for sale or rental from Teleketics, Franciscan Communications, 1229 S. Santee St., Los Angeles, CA 90015.

   The Church and Social Justice, a filmstrip with cassette and study guide. Available from Ikonographics through The Winston-Seabury Press. Phone the toll-free number, 1-800-328-5125.

2. Divide the parents into discussion groups (as in Number 2, Session 1).

*The parish's religious education coordinator or the person directing the Sacrament of Reconciliation program chairs these sessions.

3. **Discussion Questions:**
   - How do the Beatitudes and Works of Mercy differ from the values of society today?
   - Which Beatitudes or Works of Mercy are the most difficult to live?
   - What are practical ways of living the Beatitudes and Works of Mercy in our families?

4. Remind the parents that Lesson 6 concerns the Works of Mercy. Go through this lesson with the parents (20–30 minutes).

5. Bring the parents and children together for the Beatitude Badge Ceremony.

The Rite of Reconciliation

SESSION 4 (120 minutes)

1. Welcome the parents and begin with a talk on reconciliation or with one of the Suggested Resources (20–30 minutes):

   Suggested Resources:

   The Sacrament of Reconciliation, by Joseph M. Champlin. A videotape of three 30-minute segments. Available from Argus Communications, P.O. Box 7000, One DLM Park, Allen, TX 75002.

   Penance, one of 10 filmstrips in the series *Signs of Life: Celebrating Sacraments.* Available from Our Sunday Visitor, 200 Noll Plaza, Huntington, IN 46750.

   Why Go to Confession?, a 32-page booklet by Joseph M. Champlin. Available, with discount on quantities, from Franciscan Communications, 1229 S. Santee St., Los Angeles, CA 90015.

   Penance: Sacrament of Peace, Patrick Mooney. A filmstrip with record or cassette and guide. Available from Twenty-Third Publications, P.O. Box 180, Mystic, CT 06355.

   The Way Home—Reconciliation Storyscope, a film or videotape, for sale or rental, from Franciscan Communications, 1229 S. Santee St., Los Angeles, CA 90015.

2. Divide into small groups (as in Session 1, Number 2).

3. **Discussion Questions:**
   - How can the Rite of Reconciliation be a positive experience for us today?
   - How can our example show our children the need for the Sacrament of Reconciliation?
   - Where can we find continued updated material on the Sacrament of Reconciliation?

4. Lesson 8 is the last to be done at home.
   - Go through this lesson with the parents (20–30 minutes).
   - Encourage the parents to receive the Sacrament of Reconciliation when they bring their children to the penance service.

5. Bring the parents and children together.
   - Show a filmstrip on the Rite of Reconciliation. You may wish to use the same material as was shown to the parents at the beginning of this session.
   - Close the session with the Reconciliation Badge Prayer Service.

THE TEN COMMANDMENTS

1. **I am the Lord, your God. Do not have other gods.**
   - God must be important to us—more important than work, family, friends, money. We are to love God above *ALL* things.

2. **Do not misuse God's name.**
   - God's name is holy. We should say it with love and respect.

3. **Keep holy the Lord's Day.**
   - We are to use the Lord's Day to remember the goodness of God and to give thanks and praise in word and action.

4. **Honor your parents.**
   - Children are to show respect and love to parents.
   - Parents are to show love, respect, and concern for their aging parents.

5. **Do not harm yourself or others.**
   - This Commandment asks us to show respect to all people, to harm no one, and to care for our own health.

6. **Be faithful to your husband or wife.**
   - This Commandment originally meant that a man could not take a wife from a man who was already married. Today the Commandment stresses the fidelity of both parties in a marriage, as well as respect for the beauty of our sexuality and the sexuality of others.

7. **Do not steal.**
   - This Commandment forbids all forms of stealing, such as gossip (stealing someone's good name), shoplifting, cheating, taking the belongings, ideas, etc. of another.

8. **Do not lie.**
   - This Commandment forbids all forms of falsehood in word or action.

9. **Do not covet someone's husband or wife.**

10. **Do not covet someone's goods.**
    - The last two Commandments tell us that it is wrong to *plan in our mind* how to take something that belongs to another. It is not wrong to desire the belongings of another. It *is* wrong to plan to steal them or to become obsessed with wanting them.

Study Questions

Lesson 1

1. Why are you happy that you were born?
   - I am happy that I was born because I am a good person with many talents that make me special.

2. When did you become a member of the Church?
   - I became a member of the Church when I was baptized.

Lesson 2

1. In what church were you baptized?
   - I was baptized in _____ Church.

2. What can you celebrate because of your baptism?
   - I can celebrate God's life and love within me.

3. What can I say to people when I do not show love to them?
   - I can say, "I am sorry."

Lesson 3

1. Why should we live according to the Ten Commandments?
   - The Commandments help us love and care for one another.

2. What are the first five Commandments?
   - They are:
     1. I am the Lord, your God. Do not have other gods.
     2. Do not misuse God's name.
     3. Keep holy the Lord's Day.
     4. Honor your parents.
     5. Do not harm yourself or others.

3. Why do we go to Church on Sunday?
   - We go to Church to give thanks to our God who loves us.

4. What do our parents need from us?
   - They need our love, our respect, and our prayers.

Lesson 4

1. What are the last five Commandments?
   - They are:
     6. Be faithful to your husband or wife.
     7. Do not steal.
     8. Do not lie.
     9. Do not covet someone's husband or wife.
     10. Do not covet someone's goods.

2. What happens when we steal?
   - When we steal, we take something that does not belong to us.

3. What does "covet" mean?
   - To covet means we want something so much that we plan how to steal it from another.

Lesson 5

1. What is the reward promised all people who live as Jesus taught?
   - Our reward is to be happy in the Kingdom of Heaven where we see God face-to-face.

2. What do we call the eight ways Jesus gave us to be happy or blessed?
   - They are called the "Beatitudes."

Lesson 6

1. When did Jesus feed the hungry?
   - He fed a large crowd with bread and fish.

2. When Jesus lived the works of mercy, what did he teach us?
   - He taught us how to serve one another.

Lesson 7

1. What do we call actions that hurt ourselves or others?
   - We call these actions "sins."

2. What must we do after we sin?
   - We must change our hearts and become reconciled with one another and with God.

3. What is a sacrament?
   - A sacrament is a special way God touches our lives. The life and love of God is renewed in us through the sacraments.

4. What happens in the Sacrament of Reconciliation?
   - We become reconciled with those we have hurt. We ask forgiveness through the priest. We celebrate our turning back to God.

Lesson 8

1. When do we need to change our hearts?
   - We need to change our hearts when we do not live according to God's laws of love.

2. Does God get angry with us when we sin?
   - No. God does not want us to sin, but God *never* stops loving us.

3. How often can we turn back to God through the Sacrament of Reconciliation?
   - We can celebrate the Sacrament of Reconciliation over and over whenever we want to change our hearts and ask for forgiveness.

Suggested badges for
the teacher-student sessions . . .

the gentle . . . those who mourn . . . those who suffer . . . the peacemakers . . . the pure in heart . . . those who hunger and thirst for what is right . . . the poor in spirit . . .

HAPPY...

Lesson
5

MAY THE PEACE OF GOD BE WITH YOU.

will try to be
a loving
and forgiving
person.

Lesson
1

TURN AWAY FROM SIN

TURN BACK TO GOD WITH LOVING HEARTS

Lesson
7

LOVE LOVE LOVE LOVE LOVE LOVE LOVE LOVE LOVE LOVE LOVE LOVE LOVE LOVE LOVE LOVE LOVE LOVE LOVE LOVE LOVE LOVE LOVE LOVE LOVE LOVE LOVE

The laws of
God teach
me to
love.

Lesson
3